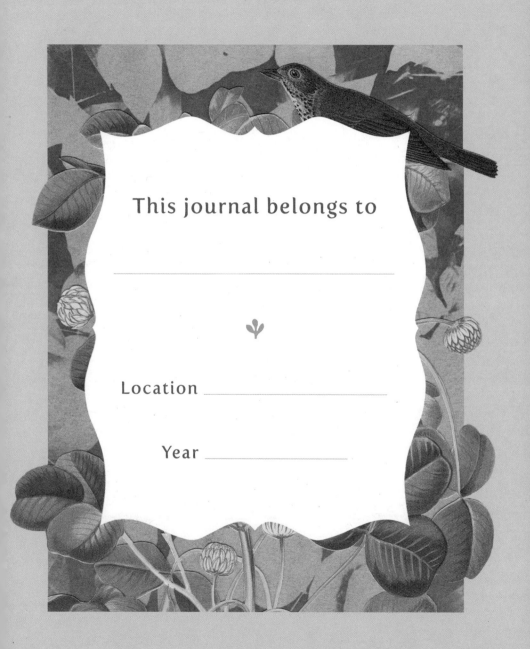

This journal belongs to

_____

❧

Location _____

Year _____

Books by Margaret Renkl

The Comfort of Crows:
A Backyard Year

Graceland, At Last: Notes on Hope and
Heartache From the American South

Late Migrations: A Natural
History of Love and Loss

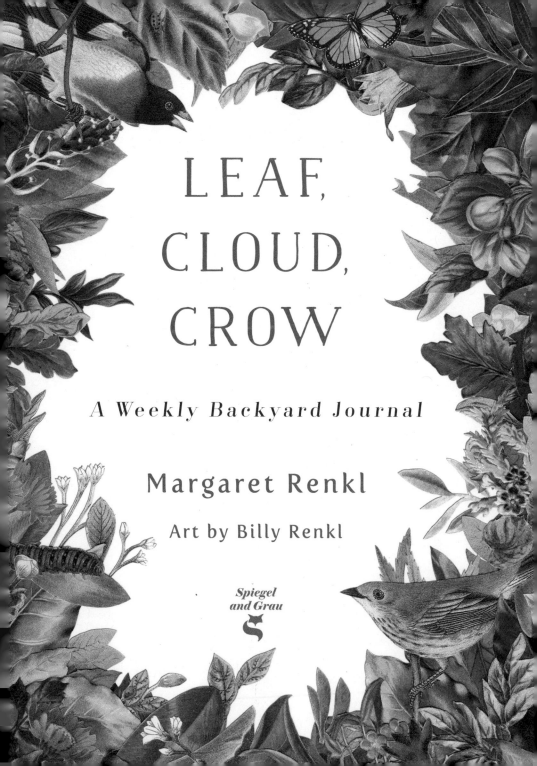

LEAF, CLOUD, CROW

A Weekly Backyard Journal

Margaret Renkl

Art by Billy Renkl

Spiegel
and Grau

S&G

Spiegel & Grau, New York
www.spiegelandgrau.com

Interior design by Meighan Cavanaugh, with art by Billy Renkl
adapted from *The Comfort of Crows: A Backyard Year*

Library of Congress Cataloging-in-Publication Data Available Upon Request

ISBN 978-1954118522 (hardcover)

Printed in Canada
Leaf, Cloud, Crow is FSC certified. It is printed on chlorine-free paper made
with 100% post-consumer waste. It uses only vegetable- and soy-based ink.

First Edition
10 9 8 7 6 5 4 3 2 1

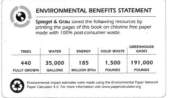

ENVIRONMENTAL BENEFITS STATEMENT

Spiegel & Grau saved the following resources by printing the pages of this book on chlorine free paper made with 100% post-consumer waste.

TREES	WATER	ENERGY	SOLID WASTE	GREENHOUSE GASES
440 FULLY GROWN	35,000 GALLONS	185 MILLION BTUs	1,500 POUNDS	191,000 POUNDS

Environmental impact estimates were made using the Environmental Paper Network Paper Calculator 4.0. For more information visit www.papercalculator.org

FSC
www.fsc.org
MIX
Paper | Supporting responsible forestry
FSC® C016245

CONTENTS

INTRODUCTION

As a child in the green woods of Alabama, I spent a lot of time doing what pretty much all children do when they're allowed to explore without adult interference. I turned over rocks and studied the creatures who dwelt in that damp darkness. I waded in creeks and felt tiny fish nibbling the freckles on my legs. When I saw a bird carrying pine straw into a tree, I learned where to look for a hidden nest. I built miniature houses of bark and sticks and moss, and I imagined the toads' delight at finding the homes I'd made for them.

I also spent a lot of time wondering how I could keep from becoming the kind of adult that nearly all the adults around me seemed to be: people who spent their days in buildings and cars. I didn't want to be a farmer like my grandfather—I disliked smelly, noisy tractors—but what else could I be and still spend my days among plants and animals? I knew I wasn't methodical enough (or mathematical enough) to be a scientist. I wasn't curious enough about the insides of animals to be a large-animal veterinarian like my heroes Dixie Cline and James Herriot. Zookeeper was out—I couldn't bear to keep an animal in a cage. What was there left to become?

It finally dawned on me that a person doesn't need to be a professional *anything* to live in a state of profound love for the natural world. In nearly forty years of professional life, I have been a teacher, a poet, a journalist, an editor, and an essayist. During all those years, no matter what work I was doing for a paycheck, I have also been a window-gazer. I have thrown my door open to storms. I have walked around in springtime, looking for wildflowers and nest-builders. I have always known when the hummingbirds set off on their travels in fall.

Before I was a writer, I was an observer, and I still think of myself as an observer first. Every day I go outside and spend at least a little time tuning out the distractions and responsibilities of my life. But even as someone whose work frequently involves writing about the natural world, it can be a struggle to make time for those moments of peace. Always there are bills to pay and laundry to fold and meals to prepare and emails to answer. Hundreds and hundreds and hundreds of emails to answer. It isn't always easy to give myself over to the timeless beauty outside my window. But when I do, I am rewarded a hundredfold. I emerge calmer, stiller, happier. I remember why I'm really here.

For nearly three decades, I have studied the creatures and plants who share this half-acre lot in suburban Nashville. Day by day, week by week, season by season, I have come to understand them more intimately, and to love them more fully. I love the broadhead skink, who suns herself on my front stoop. The crows, who are always talking with one another. The mole, who loosens the soil and makes of it a soft landing place for wildflower seeds. I love the curling passion vine, and I love the orange caterpillars who need the passion vine to survive.

In paying attention to my wild neighbors, I am learning all the ways in which I belong to a world that is so much bigger than I am. It's a gift to be reminded that I am a creature, too. It's a gift to slow down, to be quiet and alert. Paying attention can be a way of slowing time. Is there any gift more precious to a mortal being than the gift of time?

The older I grow, the more the natural world offers the gift of memory, too. When I watch a bluebird peering into one of my nest boxes, I see that unique bluebird, but I also see every other bluebird I've observed from my front window. When I wait in springtime for tadpoles to appear in my stock-tank ponds, I remember the years when my sons were boys searching for tadpoles in watery buckets, too. When I'm pulling weeds, I can still see my mother kneeling beside the front walk to plant the lilies she'd dug up from her flower beds at my childhood home—the same lilies that first came from her own childhood home and from my grandmother's childhood home before that. For me, the natural world will always be shot through with memories of the beloved human world.

But there's no denying the risks that come with noticing. When you pay attention to the natural world, you may see things that are painful to witness. A wasp carrying off a caterpillar in pieces to feed its babies, or a vibrant redbird killed by an ice storm. And the more closely you pay attention to the plants and creatures around you, the more you will notice all the ways that human life is making their lives infinitely harder.

I'm talking about climate change, of course. But I'm also talking about rodenticides and herbicides and insecticides. I'm also talking about leaves blown into piles and stuffed into bags when they could be sheltering insects for winter. I'm talking about the fashionable flowers that feed no bees and the fashionable trees that feed no birds and the fashionable lawns that feed nobody at all. In the mess we've made of the natural world, paying attention can break your heart.

And yet we must pay attention, for paying attention is what can give us the will to change—as individuals and as engaged members of our communities. One of my most fervent beliefs is that it is not too late to change, to make a difference. We can still save ourselves and our wild neighbors, but change begins with looking directly at what's happening. First love, then heartbreak, and finally action. And always, always hope.

This journal is meant to help you pay close, sustained attention to the natural world in whatever form you have access to it. I spent much of my childhood on a farm in rural Alabama and much of it in Birmingham apartment complexes. As a graduate student, I lived in the city of Philadelphia and in the city of Columbia, South Carolina. I have now lived most of my adult life in a first-ring sub-urb of Nashville. All those places have teemed with wildlife of one kind or another.

Some of us have yards or gardens. Some of us have city parks or sidewalk trees or balcony flowers. The luckiest have fields and forests and running creeks just outside our doors. We all have a sky full of birds to watch as they make their unfathomable migrations from one hemisphere to another on fragile wings. Wherever we are, we can learn to pay better attention to the wild life around us. And we can become better neighbors to other species, too.

This journal features space for you to make notes about what you observe. Those notes can take many forms: lists of plants or animals you encountered that week, observations of one creature's behavior, the temperature and humidity that day, unusual weather patterns, and so on. When you are observing the natural world, the possibilities are truly endless. Every living thing is changing every living day.

In this space you'll also find passages from *The Comfort of Crows*, my account of a year in my yard, as well as writing prompts that are based on the questions I explored during the same week of the year. Some prompts are meant to guide your observations—what you see, what you hear—while others are intended to inspire reflection or nudge memories. In the process, I hope you will fall in love with your wild neighbors the way I have fallen in love with mine. With any luck, that love will link you to other loves in your life. When we work to save our wild neighbors, we are working to save ourselves.

For me, the best thing about writing is that it makes me focus my attention on a subject more intently than anything else in my life does. Give me a test or a puzzle, and my mind wanders. Give me a notebook and pen, and I'm all in.

Writing about the natural world makes me feel more deeply connected to every living thing, and to the past and the future, too. I am no longer a child in the green woods of Alabama, but when I'm watching a wren bringing leaves to the nest she's building in the mesh bag where I keep my clothespins, I feel the same way I did the first time I watched a bird build a nest. Filled with wonder. Filled to the very brim with wonder.

HOW TO USE
THIS JOURNAL

This weekly journal covers one full year, but it doesn't start with January 1. *Leaf, Cloud, Crow* is organized by season—allowing you to track changes and cycles in the natural world and in your own life—and so it begins with the winter solstice, the first day of the season and the shortest day of the year.

If you're picking this book up later in winter, or in another season altogether, just turn to the current week and start there, circling back to the preceding weeks during the next calendar year. That's the thing about seasons: they always come back around.

Each week, you will find a quote from *The Comfort of Crows*, a related writing prompt, and plenty of room for your response. You will also find a page left blank. In this space you can make shorter notes, sketch something that caught your eye, or simply list your observations of the natural world that week, whether you're noticing new wildflowers coming up in your yard, a bird appearing during its seasonal migration, or an unexpected spring snowstorm. For tips and ideas to help you get started, keep reading.

HOW TO PAY ATTENTION

Silence and stillness are your greatest tools as a naturalist. Take care not to frighten anybody. Sit quietly and let the world come to you. Trying to get close to a wild animal will only distress it. A good pair of binoculars can help you avoid the temptation to engage in a futile chase.

The creatures who live in your ecosystem evolved to eat plants that are native to your region. To bring wild creatures closer, set a banquet for them by planting the foods they need. Keep in mind that a garden can be as large or as small as you have room for and energy to maintain. A few patio pots filled with native wildflowers will bring the bees and butterflies more surely than a whole garden filled with plants that our native insects don't recognize as food. Do a bit of research: What native plants would wild creatures in your area be especially drawn to?

If you want to deepen your knowledge of nature, you can start by collecting a few good field guides and downloading a few good apps on your phone to help you identify what you observe. (You might start with books about the wildflowers, birds, and insects of your region.) Apps rely on the clarity of photos and can't always provide a definitive ID, but they will get you in the ballpark. Then the books can help you find the name of the specific creature or plant you're looking for.

Bird feeders can be a great resource for studying your avian neighbors at close range, but they must be kept scrupulously clean to prevent the spread of diseases. And it's best not to feed other wildlife at all. Birds naturally seek out a variety of foods, but other animals may become reliant on their human feeders and lose the instinct for foraging. Special note: if you live in bear country, don't put up a bird feeder!

For wild food to be safe for wildlife, it must be kept free of poisons. Make a commitment to keep your outdoor spaces as natural as your municipal codes will allow. No chemical fertilizer. No herbicides. No pesticides. Wildflowers commonly considered weeds are crucial food sources for insects, and insects are crucial food sources for birds, reptiles, amphibians, and even mammals. Welcome insects to your outdoor spaces, and you'll be welcoming the whole wild world.

Another way to welcome your wild neighbors: Provide places for vulnerable creatures to nest, to shelter when it's cold, and to hide when predators are on the prowl. Leave the leaves where they fall, if possible, or use them as natural mulch in your flower beds and foundation plantings if codes won't allow you to leave them everywhere. Install nest boxes (with a snake baffle!) to help make up for the loss of natural nesting sites for cavity dwellers like bluebirds and chickadees and tufted titmice. Build a brush pile—ideally in a place that's unobtrusive to your human neighbors but still visible from your own window—instead of hauling brush to the street to be carted to the landfill.

Consider what you already know about the seasons and begin to check deliberately for what you might expect to find at that time of year:

In winter: Look for signs of life that you can see now, while the trees are bare, but that are invisible during the green seasons. When you see last summer's nests in the bare branches, you'll know what to watch for during nesting season next spring. Are there any sleepy animals coming out to take the sun on unseasonably warm days? What are your wild neighbors eating now? Who is carrying off the fallen leaves to line their winter dens or nests?

In spring: Look for migrating geese, cranes, and hawks heading north. (And watch for them heading south again in fall.) Songbirds migrate mainly at night, but you might see them coming down in early morning to feed and rest, especially if there are insects and berries and a clean water source in your yard or in the parks nearby. Take note of any new birds passing through, any winter residents who have departed for northern latitudes, and any summer residents who are suddenly back in town after spending winter farther south. What wildflowers have started popping up? What early bees are feeding on the flowers?

In summer: If you don't already have a bird bath, now is a great time to get one—or several—because in hot, dry weather, wild creatures have a harder time finding clean water than they have finding food. A water source on a pedestal for birds, plus another on the ground for other creatures, can bring many animals into view. What insects can you see now? What can you hear now? Late summer is high butterfly season; have you begun to see your own populations grow?

In fall: Which berries and nuts and drupes are ripening now? Which fall wildflowers have begun to bloom? Which foods do animals seem to prefer in this season of abundance? Which birds are passing through again? Which old friends have come back, and which are now on their way south?

The more you learn about seasonal activity, the more you will know what to look for—or to listen for—at every time of year. And the more you observe, the more you will fall in love with the wild world that you belong to, too—the world whose safety is in our hands.

WHEREVER YOU ARE, STOP WHAT YOU'RE DOING

From *The Comfort of Crows:*
A Backyard Year

S top and look at the tangled rootlets of the poison ivy vine climbing the locust tree. Notice the way they twist around each other like plaits in a golden braid, like tendrils of sea-weed washed to shore. Stop and look, but do not touch. Never, never touch, not even in winter.

Stop and ponder the skeleton of the snakeroot plant, each twig covered in tiny brown stars. The white petals, once embraced by bees, have dried to powder and now dust the forest floor, but here are the star-shaped sepals that held those fluffs of botanical celebration. Bend closer. Here and there are a few black seeds the goldfinches neglected to glean. Only a few, but enough.

Stop and listen to the ragged-edged beech leaves, pale specters of the winter forest. They are chattering ghosts, clattering amid the bare branches of the other hardwoods. Wan light pours through their evanescence and burnishes them to gleaming. Deep in the gray, sleeping forest, whole beech trees flare up into whispering creatures made of trembling gold.

Stop and consider the deep hollows of the persimmon's bark, the way the tree has carved its own skin into neat rectangles of sturdy protection. See how the lacy lichens have found purchase in the channels, sharing space in the hollows. Tree and lichen belong to one another. Neither is causing the other any harm.

Stop and peer at the hummingbird nest, smaller than your thumb, in the crook of the farthest reach of an oak branch. Remember the whir of hummingbird wings. Remember the green flash of hummingbird light.

Stop and notice how closely the human teenagers resemble the whistling, clicking, preening starlings.

Stop and contemplate the hollow-boned ducks floating on the water like leaves. Like deadwood. Turtles, too, drift in the sunny water. See the way the bones in the turtle's webbed foot resemble the bones in the duck's webbed foot. Hold open your hand. Trace the outline of your fingers.

Stop and think for a time about kinship. Think for a long time about kinship.

The world lies before you, a lavish garden. However hobbled by waste, however fouled by graft and tainted by deception, it will always take your breath away.

We were never cast out of Eden. We merely turned from it and shut our eyes. To return and be welcomed, cleansed and redeemed, we are only obliged to look.

Because nature is not a place to
visit. Nature is who we are.

–Ada Limón, *You Are Here:*
Poetry in the Natural World

WINTER

Winter ❧ Week 1

DECEMBER 21–27

"Nothing in nature exists as a metaphor,
but human beings are reckless metaphor
makers anyway, and only a fool could
fail to find the lesson here."

Observe the behavior of something in the natural world: dead leaves carried on the wind, perhaps, or clouds moving across the sky, or a wild creature living nearby. Is there a metaphor here for something you are pondering in your own life?

_____

_____

_____

_____

_____

_____

_____

_____

_____

_____

_____

_____

_____

_____

_____

_____

_____

Notes and Sketches

Winter ❦ Week 2

DECEMBER 28–JANUARY 3

"According to birding tradition, the first bird you see on the first day of the new year sets the tone for your next twelve months."

I dentify the first bird you see on New Year's Day. (If you don't recog- nize it, the internet or a good field guide can help.) Which of the bird's traits might be a model for the coming year? How will you work toward developing that characteristic?

_____

_____

_____

_____

_____

_____

_____

_____

_____

_____

_____

_____

_____

_____

_____

_____

_____

_____

_____

Notes and Sketches

Winter ❧ Week 3

JANUARY 4-10

"The fox vanishes. It is not a fox. It is a
blur of falling leaves, red and gold. A
phantom rush of wildness. A mirage
of a miracle, pungent and swift."

C losely observe an animal outdoors. Describe it using as many sensory details as you can. What does it look like? Sound like? Smell like? Does it remind you of any other creature or natural phenomenon you've observed?

_____

_____

_____

_____

_____

_____

_____

_____

_____

_____

_____

_____

_____

_____

_____

_____

_____

_____

_____

_____

Notes and Sketches

Winter ❧ Week 4

JANUARY 11–17

"It's a good time to stay indoors, to participate in the natural world by observing it through a window."

S tudy a wild animal through a window, while it is unaware of your
presence. How does its behavior change if another member of its
own species appears? If an animal of another species appears? How do
you change, too, in response to the arrival of someone you don't know?
Or someone you do?

_____

_____

_____

_____

_____

_____

_____

_____

_____

_____

_____

_____

_____

_____

_____

_____

_____

_____

_____

_____

Notes and Sketches

Winter ❦ Week 5

JANUARY 18-24

"Year by year, the creatures who share this yard have been teaching me the value of an untidy garden."

How do the wild animals near you make use of fallen leaves? Of dried grasses? Of dead flowers? Reflect on the benefits of an untidy yard.

_____

_____

_____

_____

_____

_____

_____

_____

_____

_____

_____

_____

_____

_____

_____

_____

_____

_____

_____

_____

Notes and Sketches

Winter ❧ Week 6

JANUARY 25-31

"I need to remember that the earth, fragile as it is, remains heartbreakingly beautiful."

Make a list of beautiful things you can see right now in the nearby natural world. End each day this week by adding at least one new beautiful thing to your list. How, if at all, does pausing for beauty change the way you experience your own life?

_____

_____

_____

_____

_____

_____

_____

_____

_____

_____

_____

_____

_____

_____

_____

_____

_____

_____

Notes and Sketches

Winter 🌱 Week 7

FEBRUARY 1-7

"I was so absorbed by the task of planning for spring that I completely forgot how long the wait for true springtime would be. I was thinking about the scent of turned earth, the feel of damp soil."

In the gray days of winter, what rituals have you created to cheer yourself up? What activities keep you connected to the natural world when it's cold outside?

_____

_____

_____

_____

_____

_____

_____

_____

_____

_____

_____

_____

_____

_____

_____

_____

_____

_____

_____

Notes and Sketches

Winter ❧ Week 8

FEBRUARY 8-14

"I am learning that it is possible to want two contrary things at once. I want nothing to change. I want everything to change."

W hat are you most eager for spring to bring? What will you miss most about winter? Does this paradox apply metaphorically to any other transition you're facing?

_____

_____

_____

_____

_____

_____

_____

_____

_____

_____

_____

_____

_____

_____

_____

_____

_____

_____

_____

_____

Notes and Sketches

FEBRUARY 15–21

"Out of nothing more than hope, I did a little more clicking around online and brought myself back to believing I had an owl pellet on my hands, and a really large one at that."

Have you ever thought you were seeing one thing in nature only to realize later that you were seeing something else entirely? Write about a time when you were completely confused by something in the natural world.

_____

_____

_____

_____

_____

_____

_____

_____

_____

_____

_____

_____

_____

_____

_____

_____

_____

_____

_____

_____

_____

Notes and Sketches

Winter ❧ Week 10

FEBRUARY 22-28

"I don't know what the crows are saying to the other crows, but I like to listen in. It's a gift to watch them living their intricate lives so visibly while the trees are bare."

L ook into the bare branches of a tree. What can you see in winter that you might not be able to see in other seasons? How can you let that knowledge affect what you look for during the other seasons?

_____

_____

_____

_____

_____

_____

_____

_____

_____

_____

_____

_____

_____

_____

_____

_____

_____

_____

_____

_____

_____

_____

Notes and Sketches

Winter 🌱 Week 11

MARCH 1-7

*"All endings are also beginnings. That is
what I tell myself again and again."*

What seems to be coming to an end in the natural world near you? What signs of new life are beginning to reveal themselves? Is there a symbol here that you can take to heart?

_____

_____

_____

_____

_____

_____

_____

_____

_____

_____

_____

_____

_____

_____

_____

_____

_____

_____

_____

_____

Notes and Sketches

Winter ❧ Week 12

MARCH 8-14

"The world is burning, and there is no time to put down the water buckets. For just an hour, put down the water buckets anyway."

S pend one full hour poking around outside without your phone in hand. How do you experience time when you spend it immersed in the natural world, far from screens? Write about the difference between screen time and nature's time.

_____

_____

_____

_____

_____

_____

_____

_____

_____

_____

_____

_____

_____

_____

_____

_____

_____

_____

_____

Notes and Sketches

Winter ❧ Week 13

MARCH 15-21

"As the pond fills, the wood frogs and
the pickerel frogs will arrive, and the
spring peepers. Their mating songs will
turn the spring nights into symphonies."

Go outdoors after nightfall and spend some time just listening. Do you hear any creatures singing? Can you identify the singers by their songs? If so, write about the singers. If not, write about the songs.

_____

_____

_____

_____

_____

_____

_____

_____

_____

_____

_____

_____

_____

_____

_____

_____

_____

_____

_____

_____

_____

Notes and Sketches

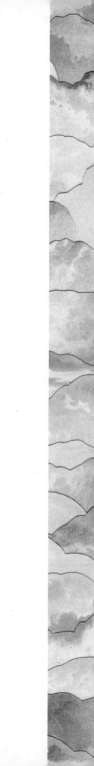

Goldfinches, dragonflies, rabbits, pine siskins. Learning all these names took me years. Learning a name for the joy of this grounding may take a lifetime.

–Camille T. Dungy, *Soil: The Story of a Black Mother's Garden*

SPRING

Spring 🌱 Week 1

MARCH 22-28

"The world understands us. We understand nothing, control less."

Human activities affect many other living things in our shared habitat, and animals are always studying our patterns. In what ways does the natural world understand us? In what ways do we fail to understand the natural world?

Notes and Sketches

Spring ❧ Week 2

MARCH 29–APRIL 4

"I try to imagine the primeval chestnut forest
and the creatures who made it their home,
the timber wolves and panthers driven from
our lands as the forests fell, creatures kept
away now by our controlling fears."

Look around you. Imagine what this landscape looked like a hundred years ago, a thousand years ago. What do you picture? What will this world look like a hundred years from now?

Notes and Sketches

Spring ❧ Week 3

APRIL 5-11

"I embrace the old-timey plants that evolved to feed wildlife, the plants with names that change from place to place and people to people. What you call the wildflowers will tell you who you are."

Can you think of a plant that goes by multiple names or nicknames? What name did you grow up calling it? When you see it blooming now, in life or in photos, what memories does it call to mind?

_____

_____

_____

_____

_____

_____

_____

_____

_____

_____

_____

_____

_____

_____

_____

_____

_____

_____

_____

_____

_____

Notes and Sketches

Spring 🌱 Week 4

APRIL 12-18

*"I demonstrated the way a bird can sit
on fragile eggs without breaking them:
the careful adjustment of world-shaped
eggs, the embrace of sheltering wings."*

The spring songbird migration is well underway now. Have you noticed any new visitors in the trees? Have some familiar winter friends suddenly disappeared? Are the local birds showing any signs of nesting activity? Does this flurry of activity—traveling, preparing, expanding, changing—mimic anything you see in your own life? In the life of your community?

_____

_____

_____

_____

_____

_____

_____

_____

_____

_____

_____

_____

_____

_____

_____

_____

_____

Notes and Sketches

Spring 🌱 Week 5

APRIL 19-25

"Wildflower seeds are carried on the wind, on the coats of animals, and in the digestive tracts of birds. Anybody paying attention would see them for the gifts they are: flowers that arrive, through no effort, to feed the bees and the butterflies."

Take a walk and look for the plants that most people call weeds. Is it possible to think of them as gifts? Does changing what you call them change your relationship to them in any way?

_____

_____

_____

_____

_____

_____

_____

_____

_____

_____

_____

_____

_____

_____

_____

_____

_____

_____

_____

_____

_____

_____

_____

_____

Notes and Sketches

Spring ❧ Week 6

APRIL 26–MAY 2

*"A running creek in springtime calls to
a child as irresistibly as it calls to any
wild creature looking for a watery
place to lay her eggs."*

Think back to your childhood. What were your favorite places in nature? What made those places feel special to you?

_____

_____

_____

_____

_____

_____

_____

_____

_____

_____

_____

_____

_____

_____

_____

_____

_____

_____

_____

_____

_____

_____

_____

Notes and Sketches

Spring ❦ Week 7

MAY 3–9

"Even when it is pointed in the right direction, a camera has a way of stunting sight. How truly valuable is a device that makes you take your eyes from an experience so momentary you might miss it altogether?"

There are advantages and disadvantages to having a camera in your pocket when you're spending time in the natural world. What do you gain when you photograph something in nature? What might you miss by pulling out your phone to take a picture?

Notes and Sketches

Spring 🌱 Week 8

MAY 10-16

"Then one squirrel, bolder than the others, moves gingerly down the nearest pine tree, pausing to shake his tail from time to time. I stop. He stops. He shakes his tail. He stops again, waiting to see if I am about to move. I don't move."

When you sit quietly outdoors, is there one squirrel or chipmunk or bird or lizard that seems bolder or bossier than the others? Is there one that seems especially timid? How much do creatures within the same species differ from one another? How much do they differ from you?

_____

_____

_____

_____

_____

_____

_____

_____

_____

_____

_____

_____

_____

_____

_____

_____

_____

_____

_____

_____

Notes and Sketches

Spring ❧ Week 9

MAY 17-23

*"I just sat there. Unmoving. Disbelieving.
It was nine o'clock on a sunny spring
morning, and a bobcat was calmly walking
to the edge of the yard and crossing the
street, right in front of my car."*

P eople often think of "wildlife" as creatures who live far from human beings, but many live right here among us, hidden from our view. What is the most surprising encounter you've had with a wild animal living in a human-dominated landscape?

Spring 🌱 Week 10

MAY 24-30

"Except when something unnatural is happening within a natural system—when a beagle grabs a baby rabbit, say, or an opossum gets caught in the crawl space—it's always best to let nature take its course, no matter how distressing its course might be."

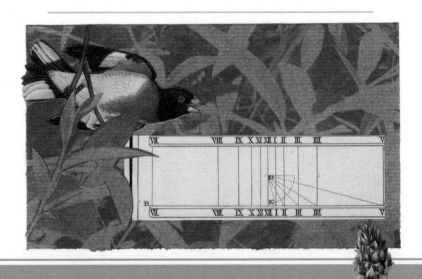

R eflect on the dangers that wild animals face every day of their lives. Have you ever witnessed something in nature that made you wish you could intervene? Have you found any way to make peace with letting nature take its course?

Notes and Sketches

Spring 🌱 Week 11

MAY 31–JUNE 6

*"The way death and life mingle and tangle,
like the passion vine that twines among
the blackberry canes in my pollinator
garden—it's always been like that."*

W hat does it mean for life and death to be entangled? In what ways is that connection upsetting to you? In what ways does it offer consolation?

_____

_____

_____

_____

_____

_____

_____

_____

_____

_____

_____

_____

_____

_____

_____

_____

_____

_____

_____

_____

_____

_____

_____

Spring ❦ Week 12

JUNE 7-13

"Now my raised beds are full of native perennials that provide nectar for bees, wasps, skippers, and butterflies, or that serve as their nurseries. I can't solve the problems of climate change, but I can plant a garden."

The troubles the natural world faces today often seem too big for the actions of any one person to make a difference, but we aren't completely powerless in the face of our wild neighbors' suffering. Reflect on the changes you've already made to help the wild creatures who live near you, or on the changes you still hope to make. How do these activities affect the way you react to bad news about the environment?

_____

_____

_____

_____

_____

_____

_____

_____

_____

_____

_____

_____

_____

_____

_____

_____

_____

_____

_____

_____

Notes and Sketches

Spring 🌱 Week 13

JUNE 14-20

"How had I allowed myself to become so busy? How long had it been since I'd spent a day in the sun, eating sandwiches from a cooler and watching water ripple across the surface of a lake?"

How long has it been since you spent an entire day in a peaceful place outdoors? Write about that day. How could you give yourself the gift of a day like that again?

_____

_____

_____

_____

_____

_____

_____

_____

_____

_____

_____

_____

_____

_____

_____

_____

_____

_____

_____

_____

_____

_____

Notes and Sketches

My pockets tell me when I've had the
best days. They burp catalpa seeds,
surrender snail shells, turn out
twigs of spicebush, fumble oak
apples round and dry.

–Joanna Brichetto, *This Is How a Robin
Drinks: Essays on Urban Nature*

SUMMER

Summer ❧ Week 1

JUNE 21–27

"A thunderstorm rolls in, and I open the
door. I pull my chair right to the jamb
and make of my house an anteroom,
a portal straddling two worlds."

Take some time this week to think about the role that weather patterns play in the natural world. How do your wild neighbors seem to respond to approaching storms? To sudden drops in temperature? To an unexpected warm spell? Do you see any parallels between your own storm preparations and theirs?

_____

_____

_____

_____

_____

_____

_____

_____

_____

_____

_____

_____

_____

_____

_____

_____

_____

_____

Notes and Sketches

Summer ❦ Week 2

JUNE 28–JULY 4

"So much of what I do in this yard is
only ever an exercise in hope."

CLASS ... AMPHIBIA: ORDER I. ANURA.   408

or less rapid ... ing ... erature: the greater the heat the more speedy is the
The ... mates the progress of the young animal.

... AND PROGRESS OF THE YOUNG FROG.

Fi ... resents th ... mbryo ... ppears several days after the e

Even when we are trying to make life a little easier for our wild neighbors, we often have no idea if our efforts are having the effect we hope for. Write the story of a time when you tried to help, not knowing if your help would be enough.

Notes and Sketches

"World, world, forgive our ignorance and
our foolish fears. For no reason but the
hope that one day we will know the
beauty of unloved things, accept
our unuttered thanks."

So many "unloved things"—creatures like mice, mosquitoes, snakes, and bats—play vital roles in our ecosystems. Think about a creature you find annoying, repulsive, or frightening. Write about the role it plays in the larger ecosystem. Does writing about it help you learn to love it a bit more?

Notes and Sketches

Summer 🌿 Week 4

JULY 12-18

"Human beings are neither vultures nor
crows. The world would count itself
lucky if we were vultures or crows."

Human beings are creatures, too, as much a part of the natural world as any other living thing. What could you do to feel more like a creature, or just a little bit closer to the earth?

Notes and Sketches

Summer ❧ Week 5

JULY 19-25

"Any blackberry ripe in the summer sun, no matter the variety, is the taste of my childhood."

W hat is the taste of childhood for you? What is the taste of summer?

Notes and Sketches

Summer ❧ Week 6

JULY 26–AUGUST 1

"I laugh at the ungainly young crows, not yet so sleek as their parents, bumbling along on the ground, croaking like frogs and stumbling like drunks."

F ind a comfortable spot outdoors to watch for fledglings just learning to fly. How can you tell which birds are juveniles? How do they
differ, in appearance and behavior, from their parents? How are they
similar?

_____

_____

_____

_____

_____

_____

_____

_____

_____

_____

_____

_____

_____

_____

_____

_____

_____

AUGUST 2-8

*"I need the words themselves to guide
me, to tell me where to go and why."*

R eflect on your own writing this year. Have any entries in this journal gone in a surprising direction? Taken you to surprising memories or observations?

_____

_____

_____

_____

_____

_____

_____

_____

_____

_____

_____

_____

_____

_____

_____

_____

_____

_____

_____

_____

Notes and Sketches

Summer ❧ Week 8

AUGUST 9–15

"Well, this is how it's meant to go,
I remind myself. In nature offspring
don't dawdle and dawdle."

When you think about the life stages you've observed among your wild neighbors, do you find any parallels to your own life? Are any of those connections worrisome? Are any reassuring?

_____

_____

_____

_____

_____

_____

_____

_____

_____

_____

_____

_____

_____

_____

_____

_____

_____

_____

_____

_____

_____

"When the world has lost its still center,
we grasp for any reminder that it is
nevertheless spinning exactly as it must."

Think back on a time when the world seemed to have lost its still center. Was there anything in the natural world that made you feel, no matter how irrationally, that all would be well somehow? Is there any natural process or phenomenon that you unconsciously turn to when you need comfort?

_____

_____

_____

_____

_____

_____

_____

_____

_____

_____

_____

_____

_____

_____

_____

_____

_____

_____

_____

_____

Notes and Sketches

AUGUST 23-29

"We have come to August, a time when summer
has gone on for so long that winter is scarcely
a memory. This is the time of summer
when summer tells us it will never end."

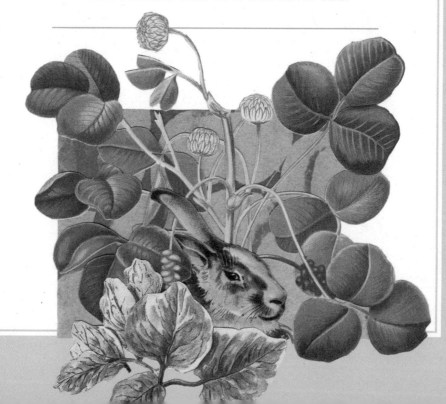

Here in the high heat of summer, take special note of the weather, the plants, and the animals around you. What early signs can you find, even now, of the coming fall? How do your wild neighbors approach the seasonal changes that are on their way?

_____

_____

_____

_____

_____

_____

_____

_____

_____

_____

_____

_____

_____

_____

_____

_____

_____

_____

_____

_____

_____

_____

_____

Notes and Sketches

AUGUST 30–SEPTEMBER 5

"Abundance is the story of approaching
autumn, in our lives and in our yard."

W hat signs of abundance—seeds, berries, acorns, drupes—can you find in the natural world surrounding you? What signs of abundance can you find in your own life right now? (Feel free to squint a little if you need to.)

_____

_____

_____

_____

_____

_____

_____

_____

_____

_____

_____

_____

_____

_____

_____

_____

_____

_____

_____

Notes and Sketches

Summer ❧ Week 12

SEPTEMBER 6–12

"I think of the marvelous compound eye
of the housefly, creating a mosaic from
thousands of images. For a housefly, the
world is a work of collage art, patched
together but whole and hopelessly,
extravagantly beautiful."

We can't truly understand the experience of other creatures, but we can learn something from trying to imagine life as they live it. Take a moment to consider another living being—perhaps one that you've been documenting in this journal. In what ways does it seem to experience the world differently than you do?

Notes and Sketches

SEPTEMBER 13–19

"I watched that hummingbird hunched down
in a cold rain, resolute and undefeated,
preparing in his unconscious way for a journey
whose dangers he couldn't predict, and I
thought, 'I should be more like that.' Flexible,
adaptable, untraumatized by change."

In one way of looking at it, we are all on a journey whose dangers we cannot predict. The difference between a hummingbird and a human being is that we worry at times about the unknown future while the hummingbird—as far as we know, at least—does not. Is there a lesson here? How has the capacity for worry been a benefit to you? How has it been a hindrance?

_____

_____

_____

_____

_____

_____

_____

_____

_____

_____

_____

_____

_____

_____

_____

_____

_____

Notes and Sketches

The calendar says fall. The sun says
summer is done—an equinox has
come. Still, the heat climbs to make
me think of June. Confused, I turn to
the wild things. They all agree—it is
the season for which we have no name.

–J. Drew Lanham, "Come Autumn"

FALL

Fall ❧ Week 1

SEPTEMBER 20-26

"I have to work to love September, that
in-between time when the heavy heat
lingers but the maple leaves have already
started to turn. In the garden, only the
zinnias are still blooming, and even they
are shabby and dusted with mildew."

Is there a time of year that you struggle to love? If you focus on it more deliberately, looking for something about this time of year that is beautiful or inspiring, what comes to mind?

Notes and Sketches

Fall  *Week 2*

SEPTEMBER 27–OCTOBER 3

*"Autumn light is the loveliest light there
is. Soft, forgiving, it makes all the
world a brightened dream."*

Each day this week, pick a time to spend a few moments observing the light. How would you describe the light of autumn? Does it change at all from one day to the next?

Notes and Sketches

Fall 🌱 Week 3

OCTOBER 4-10

"That night-blooming cereus brought my grandmother back to me in her halo of white hair. It brought back, too, her plum tree, long since cut down, and the feeling of red dirt between my toes. For an hour, just this once, it made me remember what it feels like when the world is exactly as it must be, and I am exactly where I belong."

A re there any plants or animals that you associate strongly with memories of a loved one? Any seasonal changes that make you remember home with an ache?

_____

_____

_____

_____

_____

_____

_____

_____

_____

_____

_____

_____

_____

_____

_____

_____

_____

_____

_____

_____

Notes and Sketches

Fall ❧ Week 4

OCTOBER 11–17

"Relief is on the way, the forecast tells
us, but the most we have had of autumn
so far is the right slant of light, for this
year the mild October light has not
brought the usual mild temperatures."

C limate change has disrupted seasonal rhythms in addition to bringing more extreme weather. What has fall been like so far in your area? How does it compare to recent autumns? To those in more distant memory?

_____

_____

_____

_____

_____

_____

_____

_____

_____

_____

_____

_____

_____

_____

_____

_____

_____

_____

_____

_____

_____

_____

Notes and Sketches

Fall ❦ Week 5

OCTOBER 18-24

*"There's a brilliance to the bloody,
perilous world. Sometimes the creatures
who survive are the fittest. Sometimes
they are merely the luckiest."*

So many things that happen in nature are very hard to watch. Snakes eat baby birds. Hawks eat snakes. Even tiny hummingbirds engage in fierce aerial battle. Think of some natural phenomenon that was very hard for you to watch. Write about its bloody brilliance.

Notes and Sketches

Fall ❦ Week 6

OCTOBER 25-31

"What if resting, all by itself, is
the real act of holiness?"

S et aside some time this week to enter more fully into the natural world. Take a longer walk than usual, spend an hour at the pond in the park, or just sit on your own stoop and listen to the birds. Think about how you feel when you go inside. How does "resting" in the natural world differ from other ways you typically spend your time away from obligations?

_____

_____

_____

_____

_____

_____

_____

_____

_____

_____

_____

_____

_____

_____

_____

_____

_____

Notes and Sketches

NOVEMBER 1-7

"The light that renders a crow
incandescent in the afternoon is the
same light that only minutes later
tenders the gift of twilight, when colors
fade and all the world becomes a crow."

Head outside at twilight. How do the fleeting moments between daylight and darkness make the familiar feel momentarily unfamiliar? Is it possible to reframe some aspect of your own life in a way that makes you understand it anew?

_____

_____

_____

_____

_____

_____

_____

_____

_____

_____

_____

_____

_____

_____

_____

_____

_____

_____

_____

_____

_____

Fall ❦ Week 8

NOVEMBER 8-14

"To sit on a porch in the rainy woods is a bit like being a snail: inside and outside at once, at home in the wet world."

Think for a time about how rain can transform your experience of the natural world. How does the world feel different when it's damp outside? How do the natural world's smells and colors change? Is your region getting the usual fall rains this year?

_____

_____

_____

_____

_____

_____

_____

_____

_____

_____

_____

_____

_____

_____

_____

_____

_____

_____

_____

_____

_____

_____

Fall ❧ Week 9

NOVEMBER 15-21

"Take a leaf into your hand. Put it on your desk or next to your bed. Keep it nearby, through whatever troubles the long winter brings. It will help you remember that nothing is truly over."

S earch for a fallen leaf. Describe it in as much detail as you can. How can it help you remember that nothing is truly over?

_____

_____

_____

_____

_____

_____

_____

_____

_____

_____

_____

_____

_____

_____

_____

_____

_____

_____

_____

_____

_____

_____

Notes and Sketches

Fall ❧ Week 10

NOVEMBER 22-28

"More and more I ponder words like
bounty and replete and enough. I think of
what we are losing from this world and
of what we will leave behind when we
ourselves are lost. The trees. The stories."

W hat is one legacy you hope to leave behind for years to come—in the natural world and otherwise?

_____

_____

_____

_____

_____

_____

_____

_____

_____

_____

_____

_____

_____

_____

_____

_____

_____

_____

_____

_____

_____

_____

Notes and Sketches

NOVEMBER 29–DECEMBER 5

"The night sky is full of stars best seen from a

dark place. I try to remember that."

Every night this week, just before bed, walk outside and look at the sky. What can you hear? What can you see? How are these longer nights affecting you?

_____

_____

_____

_____

_____

_____

_____

_____

_____

_____

_____

_____

_____

_____

_____

_____

_____

_____

_____

_____

_____

Notes and Sketches

Fall ❧ Week 12

DECEMBER 6-12

"The understory at the park has died back now, and the contours of the land are evident once more."

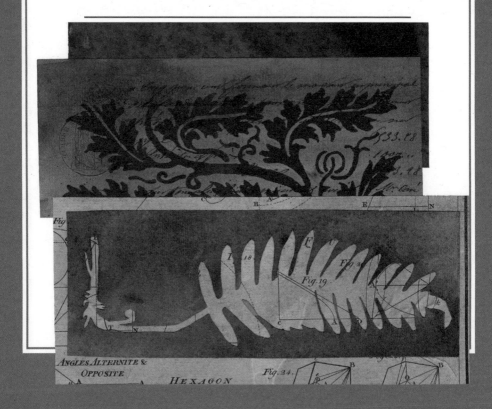

The year is coming to an end, but the stark loveliness of winter is just beginning. Which chapters are closing in your own life? Which ones are starting to open?

_____

_____

_____

_____

_____

_____

_____

_____

_____

_____

_____

_____

_____

_____

_____

_____

_____

_____

_____

Notes and Sketches

Fall ❧ Week 13

DECEMBER 13-20

"Every day I stand at my window and
watch the bluebirds. I am far from feeling
any confidence in the future, but when I
look at the busy tableau before me,
something flutters inside—something
that feels just a little bit like hope."

When you think about the plants and animals that you've been
pondering this year, what brings you the most hope?

_____

_____

_____

_____

_____

_____

_____

_____

_____

_____

_____

_____

_____

_____

_____

_____

_____

_____

_____

_____

_____

_____

_____

Notes and Sketches

IMPORTANT DATES

❧

I remember being surprised when I learned that the solstice and equinox don't occur on fixed dates. Because the Earth takes a little longer than 365 days to go around the sun, the dates of the solstices and equinoxes vary from year to year. (This is also why we have leap years every four years.) Here are those dates for easy reference. Because of these variations in timing, the first week of a season in this journal may fall slightly outside the solstice or equinox.

2024

Winter solstice: December 21

2025

Spring equinox: March 20
Summer solstice: June 20

Fall equinox: September 22
Winter solstice: December 21

2026

Spring equinox: March 20
Summer solstice: June 21
Fall equinox: September 22
Winter solstice: December 21

2027

Spring equinox: March 20
Summer solstice: June 21
Fall equinox: September 23
Winter solstice: December 21

RESOURCES

🌱

Though phones can hamper a truly immersive experience in nature, the phone's built-in camera can be a useful tool for identifying your wild neighbors without disturbing them. Zoom in, take a photo, run it through a good app, and then follow up with the appropriate entry in a detailed field guide—this is my most reliable method for learning about the world without trampling the world in the process.

Here are some sample resources to get you started, but there are many, many others, and what's available is constantly changing. Be sure to click around online for additional materials.

Apps and Websites

Many apps double as massive citizen-science projects. In addition to helping users identify plants and animals, they also help scientists collect vast amounts of data. Every uploaded photo adds to the app's database, allowing scientists to track animal populations and behavior. As you're using these apps to learn more about the wildlife around you, in other words, you're also participating in conservation efforts to save the very creatures you're learning about.

For help identifying everything:

iNaturalist

Seek

For help identifying birds:

The Cornell Lab of Ornithology (both its website and its mobile app, Merlin Bird ID)

For help identifying insects and spiders:

Picture Insect

For help identifying butterflies:

Leps by Fieldguide

For help identifying bees and wasps:

Bumble Bee Watch

Wild Bee ID

For help identifying plants:

PictureThis

PlantNet

Searchable Native Plant Databases

Gardening for wildlife takes a little more effort than driving to the nearest big-box nursery. National chains rarely carry native plants, and even many local nurseries rely heavily on plants that North American birds and insects don't recognize as food. Unless you're in a specialized local-plant nursery, you'll need to research plants that are native to your region, as well as the specific growing conditions they require, and look for local or online suppliers of seeds or seedlings. Here are some good places to start your research.

Homegrown National Park

Lady Bird Johnson Wildflower Center

National Audubon Society

National Wildlife Federation

Native Plant Trust

USDA Plants Database

Field Guides

Building a library of useful nature books can be the occupation of a lifetime—there are probably as many field guides in print as there are human beings tromping around in fields and forests on any given day. Field guides range from laminated pamphlets, ideal for beginners, to doorstop tomes that can deepen the knowledge of even the most experienced naturalist. Some field guides are region- or state-specific. Some focus on a particular type of animal. The field guides I use most often are unique to the ecosystem where I live, but I love a comprehensive generalist guide, too, especially to creatures that always seem to stump me. (Will I *ever* learn to tell sweat bees apart?)

One place to start building your collection is any library or bookstore with a wide selection of nature and wildlife titles. Once you've sampled a few, you'll have a better idea of how you prefer a field guide to be illustrated (with drawings? with photographs?), which taxonomies you find easiest to navigate, and how much detail you'd like to have at hand. Then choose the book that seems most useful for your own purposes. Or choose several, for cross-referencing.

ABOUT THE AUTHOR

Margaret Renkl is the author of *The Comfort of Crows: A Backyard Year*, *Graceland, At Last: Notes on Hope and Heartache From the American South*, and *Late Migrations: A Natural History of Love and Loss*. She is a contributing opinion writer for *The New York Times*, where her essays appear weekly. The founding editor of *Chapter 16*, a daily literary publication of Humanities Tennessee, and a graduate of Auburn University and the University of South Carolina, she lives in Nashville.

ABOUT THE ARTIST

Billy Renkl is an artist whose work has been featured in many solo and group exhibitions, including shows in Nashville, New Orleans, New York City, Cincinnati, and Berlin, Germany. He is the illustrator of *The Comfort of Crows: A Backyard Year* and *Late Migrations: A Natural History of Love and Loss*, both by Margaret Renkl, and *When You Breathe* by Diana Farid, among other projects. Like his sister, he is a graduate of Auburn University and the University of South Carolina. He lives in Clarksville, Tennessee, where he teaches at Austin Peay State University.